Chakras

The Guide To Third Eye Awakening For Psychic
Development And The Root To The Crown Chakra

*(Boost Your Positive Attitude And Develop Your Psychic
Skills)*

Jordan Cameron

TABLE OF CONTENT

Color Therapy For Chakra Clearing 1

Managing And Restoring Your Chakras 14

Hormones And The Heart Chakra 34

Saturn Resides In The Root Chakra. 49

Solar Plexus Pranayama And Yoga 71

Blue 83

Utilize Throat Chakra To Speak Your Inner Truth 104

The Heart Chakra, The Fourth Chakra. 115

Chakras And Energy Channel Varieties 127

Third Chakra 134

Chakras And Glands 137

Color Therapy For Chakra Clearing

Color therapy is a technique that can be used to help you balance your chakras. This is a truly unique technique, as it employs some of the colors we discussed previously in order to restore your chakras to their correct functioning. Each chakra will correspond to a specific color or hues, and you can use these to help you achieve the desired results. Here, we'll discuss color therapy and how you can use it to align your chakras in a straightforward manner.

Recognizing color therapy

When discussing chakras, we are referring to energy channels that will flow down the center of your body. There are seven major chakras in the body, and they will keep each other in check to the greatest extent possible. Each of these chakras will represent a distinct form of energy, and when one of them is out of balance, it can have negative effects on your mental and physical health, as well as on the other chakras.

For instance, if you suffer from seasonal affective disorder, this could be attributed to your crown chakra, which is located at the summit of your head. Or, if you are experiencing something like an imbalance within the heart chakra, it will manifest in a variety of ways, including a weakened immune system or sensitivities.

In addition to regulating your emotions and maintaining equilibrium, each chakra will be associated with a distinct hue. This is why color therapy has frequently been used to help restore some of the lost balance in the affected chakra. Some people may be skeptical of color therapy or assume it doesn't work, but you will find that wearing a pendant or bracelet of the chakra's color, or placing a gemstone of the chakra's color on the correct spot for a short time will be sufficient to provide you with the needed relief.

Here, we will devote some time to discussing the colors required for each of the chakras you wish to develop. Determine which chakra is causing you the most trouble, and then choose the appropriate color for color therapy to be effective.

The materials you require

The throne
In this case, we will need to use violet. It is very beneficial to communicate with a person's spiritual self through the violet energy's ability to connect with our emotions and thoughts. When we are able to use the violet gemstone to assist with a blocked crown chakra, we can bring out our creative side, increase our self-confidence, and even prevent melancholy.

The forehead

Indigo is the color required for the maintenance of the brow chakra. This one will assist in opening the third eye chakra in order to make you feel more intuitive and faithful to what is happening around you. You may wish to utilize indigo gemstones whenever you are dealing with intuition or space-related difficulties.

The pharynx
Following the heart chakra is the pharynx chakra. This one will be in charge of your larynx and lungs, and in addition to making things difficult in terms of your lungs' health, it can also make it more difficult for you to be trustworthy or communicate with others. The required color for the pharynx chakra is the color blue.

The center
When it comes to the heart, you want to ensure that it is sufficiently open so that you can manage the love you have for others and that it doesn't overwhelm you when you're around others. If you

need to balance the heart chakra so that it is neither overactive nor underactive, you should use green gemstones.

Solar plexus
When it comes to balancing the solar plexus chakra, the color yellow will be required. Because you will need it to increase your optimism, self-assurance, and practicality. When the solar plexus chakra is not functioning properly, it can lead to stomach issues, and you need to add more optimism and vibrancy to your life in order to feel better. The color yellow can aid in this regard.

Sacral
You will discover that the sacral chakra is situated in the lower abdomen. And when this one is not functioning properly, it is frequently due to problems with the testes, ovaries, or uterus. People are happy, self-reliant, and sociable when this is open and functioning correctly. Who wouldn't want more of that in his or her life? If you wish to increase your work with the

sacral chakra, you will need to investigate orange-colored gemstones.

The bottom
We will conclude by discussing the root chakra. When we speak of this chakra, we are referring to one that is located near the base of your vertebrae. This condition will involve the bladder, kidney, groin, legs, and spine. When it's not functioning as well as you'd like, these factors can cause a great deal of difficulty with feeling grounded. When it comes to this chakra, red is the optimal color to deal with.

As can be seen, the hues change gradually as one descends the body. You will have purple and blue near the top of your cranium, in the areas where you would like to have a great deal of calmness and composure in your thinking, heart, and relationships. As you progress down the body, you will work with colors that are hotter, evoking more passion and happiness than those above, because you want passion in your stomach, your grounding, and even your sexuality. Having the correct colors for the correct chakras will make all the difference in how well the chakras function for you.

Beginning the use of color therapy

Now that we've taken a brief look at the colors required to begin using color therapy in our own lives, we can move on to the next step. Some individuals choose to visit a professional, at least for the initial few sessions, in order to have color therapy administered and to feel better overall. This is an excellent method for resolving problems with your chakras and ensuring that everything is done correctly. However, you can perform color therapy on your own if you feel secure doing so or if you are unable to locate a professional who performs this therapy on their own. To get started with color therapy, you must complete the following steps:

Find a place where you can spend at least fifteen to twenty minutes alone. You should not have a lot of distractions and other items while performing this task.

Now, either on the bed or the floor, recline on your back. You should have seven fabric swatches nearby that correspond to the seven colors we discussed earlier and the seven main chakras you are working with.

When ready, close your eyes while lying down and simply unwind. To prepare, take some calm, deep breaths.

As you begin to unwind, review the day's events in reverse chronological order. Start with the current moment, when you are lying down, and work your way back to when you awoke that morning.

You must identify the main attitudes and emotions that you experienced or were exposed to in other people throughout the day as you go through these events. Consider what emotions were affected by these events, using a table if necessary.

When this evaluation is complete, you should take the color swatches for each of the identified chakras and position them on the corresponding part of the body.

As you lie on your back with these colors on your body, imagine that each color is being absorbed through the chakra. If you have selected more than one item, consider each of them separately. Focus your awareness on the color that is being absorbed so that the chakra can begin to heal more.

Ensure that you are taking steady breaths throughout this process while you are drawing the color from the swatch into the chakra, and then restore the chakra's balance. You will need to dedicate a few minutes to balancing each chakra.

After completing all of the colors, regardless of how many there are, you will be able to take a few more long breaths and then feel revitalized and energized.

Complete chakra therapy

With the preceding option, we discussed how we could assist a few chakras when they may have had a difficult day. However, if you have had a particularly difficult time or if you are new to the concept of chakras, it may be a good idea to focus on a complete body color therapy in order to strengthen all of your chakras. The following stages are required to perform this complete chakra therapy:

Place each of the previously possessed color specimens in the appropriate chakra.

Inhale deeply and allow the body to assimilate the energy of all these colors.

As you lie there and breathe in these colors, maintain your concentration on the fact that each of your chakras is being harmonized, balanced, and strengthened by the others. Feel, observe, and understand that the entire energy system is beginning to strengthen. Sense that the body is regaining its equilibrium.

You should wear these swatches for at least five to ten minutes, or until you are prepared to feel balanced, aligned, and energized before continuing with your day.

Other applications of color therapy

Some individuals are aware that they have issues with a specific chakra, so they employ a slightly different color therapy technique. With this one, we will use a pendent or a gemstone and wear it constantly, such as in a necklace or bracelet. This gemstone should match the desired color of the chakra. You can then keep this item as close to you as necessary, in some instances wearing it daily, so that you can receive the full benefits of this chakra.

When it comes to color therapy, you will discover that it is one of the simplest ways to maintain your chakras aligned and functioning properly. Whether you only need to focus on a few chakras at a time or you want to do a full-body therapy for all of your chakras, color therapy is frequently one of the best options available.

Managing And Restoring Your Chakras

Meditation for Balancing and Regulating Chakras

You have already gained knowledge of how to activate your chakras. Now is the time to discover how to control them. Always leaving your chakras completely open is dangerous. This makes them more susceptible to external vibrational patterns. These external vibrations attract forces with low frequency. When these forces enter your sphere of influence, they sap your vitality. This diminished vitality is taxing on your body's organs. To prevent this, you must adapt your physical vibrations to the natural frequency by slowing them down. Fortunately, this can be readily attained through meditation.

Sit comfortably and ensure that your weight is distributed in the center of your body. Maintain an upright back, as the chakras must be properly aligned for the energy flow to be effective.

Now, concentrate on your respiration. Consider the oxygen that is entering and exiting your body. Visualize the air moving downwards and reaching your Root chakra each time you inhale.

Imagining your Crown chakra as a conduit is the next step. Imagine a divine, liquid-white light cascading down your seventh chakra. Visualize and sense that energizing liquid light flowing from your Crown all the way to your first chakra, passing through, contacting, and recharging your sixth, fifth, fourth, third, second, and first chakras. Imagine the warmth permeating your body as this occurs.

Perform a grounding exercise when you are finished. Consider yourself as a tree developing roots. Your roots are expanding, extending, extending, and embracing the earth. You are a component of the planet. As such, you have access to its boundless source of strength and unconditional affection. Imagine your roots absorbing this vital force and transporting it to your body. It sustains you. It fortifies you. It imparts vitality and promotes growth.

Activating Your Body's Energy

Be in the center of the gathering. Imagine your energy emanating from your body and filling the space. Imagine the light illuminating every crevice.

Through the release of energy, you are balancing the chakras in this manner. This action bolsters your aura. Additionally, it allows you to contain the energies of others. The outer boundary of your aura will perceive the thoughts and emotions of other people, so they do not need to enter your space and affect your body. This protects you from intruding energies and prevents you from experiencing other people's emotions, maladies, pain, and stresses.

Reconciliation of the Chakras

It is not sufficient to activate and balance your chakras. You must also continuously restore them. It is normal to encounter a variety of negative situations on a daily basis. But every external stimulus your body experiences, no matter how small or large, results in electromagnetic changes. Each time you experience stress, your body enters a state of defense, and the resulting tension inhibits energy transmission.

Alternately, a chakra explosion could occur. As previously mentioned, when one or more of the other chakras are blocked, the remaining chakras tend to overcompensate. In response to extreme tension, these chakras may expand to a width of one foot. Consider it excess. Eventually, the chakra will absorb unassimilated and, consequently, unusable energies. As a consequence, a great deal of energy is released, leaving the body depleted. Heart and Solar Plexus chakras are commonly affected by chakra blowouts. In addition to stress, drug use can also cause charka explosions, particularly in the cranium. To determine which of your chakras are blasted out or at risk of blowing out, observe the manifestations of overactive chakras. (See Chapter 2) Inertia, a sense of congestion, and restlessness are also symptoms. Additionally, you may experience physical discomfort or pressure on the chakra. Occasionally, it feels like a pinching sensation, although each individual's experience may vary.

If you desire to measure your chakras, you will need the assistance of a third party, preferably a trained healer. The chakras may be measured by an expert using energy readings or a yardstick. He may also use a pendulum to gauge it. In the latter scenario, you will be required to recline on the ground. The other individual will then suspend the pendulum a few inches above your chakra, using his dominant hand to hold the pendulum. He will start with your first chakra, then your second, etc. A stagnant pendulum indicates an obstructed chakra. A balanced chakra will generate a natural clockwise rotation. In contrast, a blown-out chakra that is discharging an excessive amount of energy will cause the pendulum to swing in the opposite direction. A well-balanced chakra has a diameter of four to six inches. More than that constitutes an explosion. Moreover, it is essential that the diameters of all of your chakras are identical.

So, what should you do once you realize you're experiencing a blowout? Visualize the chakra returning to its normal size and placement. Place your hand three inches above the chakra and concentrate on directing the energy back towards your body when this is insufficient. Try moving your hand counterclockwise. If that does not work, attempt the opposite direction.

The presence of pain on a chakra indicates that it is closed and endeavoring to open. You may choose to assume the prescribed meditation position for that chakra. (See the preceding chapter) However, if the discomfort is severe, apply a light massage to the affected area. If this exacerbates the discomfort, the massage should be discontinued.

Find a calm place and close your eyes. Place your healing intentions in the area of discomfort. Focus your attention on the location and determine precisely how it feels. Is it warm? Is it chilly? Is this an acute or dull pain? Does the pain radiate to other regions of the body? Focus your awareness on the specific chakra to determine the cause of the blockage. It could take some time for the information to reach you. It can be an image, a recollection of an event, a message, or an emotion. If the discomfort persists following the emergence of consciousness, seek professional assistance.

In addition to meditation, other methods of pain relief include:

Placing the appropriate therapeutic crystal on a chakra

A healer will incorporate the negative energy from your chakra into his own body during Lemurian Chakra Healing. Then, he will convert it to positive energy. He will then return the energy to you through your higher chakras. (This refers to your eighth, ninth, tenth, and eleventh chakras, which are well beyond your summit chakra)

Breathwork (Pranayama) in Craniosacral Therapy

Holistic Therapy and Complementary Medicine

Reiki enhancing the element associated with the chakra (to be discussed in greater detail later).

Healing Stones

Using healing stones and crystals situated directly above the chakra is a second method for promoting chakra healing. In general, the crystal that functions best with a chakra is one whose color matches its own. However, there are no strict guidelines regarding chakra color. During meditation, you may perceive the energy manifesting as a secondary color, or you may have a completely distinct color interpretation for each chakra. For instance, the normally verdant Heart chakra is occasionally pink. In addition, it is sometimes preferable to treat a chakra with its opposite color. To comprehend what an opposite color is, consider this illustration.

Red primary color plus yellow primary color equals orange secondary color.

In this color scheme, the principal color blue is absent. Consequently, blue is the hue opposite of orange. Orange corresponds to the sacral chakra, so orange-colored stones can be used to heal it. However, you can also restore the sacral chakra with blue stones (the color's opposite).

Using a miniature pyramid to conceal the gemstone is one technique. This will ensure that the energy is contained within the pyramid and that your chakra is thoroughly cleansed. The pyramid can be constructed from simple cardboard.

First Chakra

The finest crystals for this chakra are those with a reddish hue, such as ruby, red zincite, and garnet. However, black is also a color associated with the first chakra, so healing crystals such as black obsidian, black tourmaline, and hematite can also be used.

Third Chakra

Orange and blue-green stones are the most effective for healing this chakra. Orange calcite, carnelian, blue-green turquoise, and blue-green fluorite are examples.

Throne Chakra

Use a yellow gemstone for this chakra, such as citrine, amber, golden calcite, yellow jasper, and yellow agate.

The 4th Chakra

Using pink crystals, activate, cleanse, and heal the Heart chakra. Rose quartz, cantaloupe tourmaline, and pink tourmaline are included. Additionally, you may use green crystals such as malachite, jade, and aventurine. When working with any of the chakras, it is possible to use a combination of stones. In this instance, malachite and rose quartz work well together.

The 5th Chakra

The most effective stones for activating this chakra are blue. Use turquoise, blue calcite, blue lace agate, blue kyanite, and sodalite.

The 6th Chakra

Lapis lazuli, sugilite, and azurite are the most conducive indigo stones with the Third Eye chakra.

The 7th Chakra

Utilize violet and gold-white crystals for opening, balancing, and purifying the Crown chakra. These include amethyst, white topaz, white calcite, clear quartz, and other medicinal stones with high vibrations.

Through the Senses and Elements, Chakras are Healed.

As mentioned previously, various physical elements reside in each of your seven main chakras, but each chakra is also associated with a distinct bodily sense. One method to heal a chakra is to increase its associated natural element. The chakras can also be nourished through their corresponding senses.

First Chakra

The Earth element is associated with the Root chakra. It corresponds to the sense of scent. Due to its connection with the physical body, vigorous physical exercise is an effective method for healing the first chakra. Having a direct relationship with the sense of scent, aromatherapy is another effective method for healing this chakra. In addition, lunges are recommended for maintaining a healthy Root chakra.

Third Chakra

Water is the element associated with the sacral chakra. Through aquatic therapy, you can increase the water element in your energy center to facilitate healing. The third chakra is associated with the sense of taste, so one method to nourish it would be to consume nourishing foods. This chakra benefits from cinnamon, vanilla, honey, strawberries, and other delicious fruits. Other recommended therapies include tantric yoga and hatha yoga. Included among the finest exercises for the sacral chakra are pelvic thrusts.

Throne Chakra

The element Fire is associated with the Solar Plexus chakra. Obtaining sufficient sunlight is one method for healing this chakra. As the third chakra is associated with the sense of sight, yantra and other visual therapies are recommended. To maintain a healthy Solar Plexus chakra, dance as an enjoyable form of exercise.

The 4th Chakra

The Heart chakra's element is Air. Therefore, respiration exercises are recommended. Because it is associated with the sense of touch, tons of gentle, loving touch is an effective form of therapy. Self-embraces and hugs are prescribed. Regarding fitness maintenance, cardio exercises are suggested for this chakra.

The 5th Chakra

Sound is the element associated with the Throat chakra and is correlated to the hearing sense. Therefore, sound is the most effective treatment. Regularly recite chakra mantras or listen to music that makes you joyful or relaxed. Alternately, you may choose to chant or scream as a form of release to exercise your vocal cords.

The 6th Chakra

Light, the element associated with the Third Eye chakra, is related to the Sixth

Sense. The most effective method of healing for this chakra is therapeutic imagery. Another method for enhancing this chakra is lucid dreaming.

The 7th Chakra

As the Crown chakra is located outside the corporeal body, it has no connection to any physical element or sense. However, it represents Space or Ether as well as thought. The best way to heal this chakra is through mental stillness, so make meditation a regular practice. Fasting is an additional means of nourishing your Crown chakra. Maintain its health with detox regimens. Incense containing myrrh, sage, and juniper are also beneficial for the seventh chakra.

Hormones And The Heart Chakra

We tend to speak incoherently about hormones, particularly female hormones, without comprehending what they are and how they affect the entire body.

Hormones are produced throughout the body by glands. They are chemical messengers that travel through the bloodstream and penetrate tissues, where they regulate growth, emotions, reproduction, and metabolism, as well as overall health and well-being.

A deficiency in insulin causes diabetes, a deficiency in oestrogen can cause weight gain or hot flushes, and recent research confirms that an excess of testosterone can be the cause of increased aggression in some males.

Hormones are highly potent. It only takes a small quantity to induce life-altering changes in cells or the entire body. This is why excess or deficiency of a particular hormone can be dangerous. If you have symptoms of a hormone disorder, your physician can arrange for laboratory tests to measure the hormone levels in your blood, urine, or saliva.

Similar to professional pregnancy tests, home pregnancy tests detect pregnancy hormones in urine.

In conclusion, regulated hormones are essential for a healthy system.

Each of the seven main chakras affects various glandular systems. Therefore, maintaining a balanced chakra system will automatically have a balancing effect on your hormone system.

Using Crystals for Personal Defense

How to Fend Off Attacks with Stones

Protection in the context of crystal healing refers to the act of erecting a barrier to prevent external forces, such as energy or other individuals, from invading our personal energy space. The true concept of protection goes beyond the barrier. It is the desire to discover one's own support and strength, as well as the ability to trust the outside world and be vulnerable in front of others. Crystal cannot create an actual shield, but it can help a person concentrate on the obstacles they must surmount.

Cutting Negative Energy Ties

The term "cord" is introduced as a portion of one person's energy that has become entangled in another person's energy field. It is described as a sensation of something blocking or sapping the person's energy. When energy is exchanged between people, which occurs daily, some of the energy of the other person may adhere to the recipient. This typically occurs unintentionally as part of the energy exchange process. It can even occur within the individual's family or intimate circle of friends. When a friend is going through a difficult time, for instance, we come to their aid and are frequently affected by their suffering and circumstance. This effect can be so potent that it can linger even after we depart the location. This indicates that the friend's energy has affixed itself to us, and we must rid ourselves of it. This is where cord cutters come in. It is a method of purging and purifying one's personal energy field so that the holder can resume normal daily activities.

The first step is to use the environment to purify one's energy consumption.

One method is to use sounds that can disrupt the ambient energy. For this type of cord severing, a Tibetan bell is optimal, but any bell will suffice. Because different metals produce distinct frequencies, it is recommended to use bells made from various materials. The next step is to ring the bell around the entire energy field, as hearing the sound of the bell helps to escape the negative energy field and allows the user to concentrate on regaining positive energy.

Negative energy connections can also be severed using pieces of black kyanite. Black kyanite can effectively use severe cords from friends, partners, family, coworkers, etc., but it is necessary to acquire this crystal and have a strong and distinct intention. The next step is to grasp the stone to establish a connection with it. Typically, black kyanite connects to the chakra centers, at which point the holder must close their eyes and focus into their body. The black kyanite is used to sever the cords by visualizing the removal of the negative energy once it has been identified. The holder can complete this process by visualizing himself expelling the previously extracted energy and replacing it with positive energy. The procedure must be repeated until all negative energy has been eliminated.

Occasionally, this type of behavior can result in physical effects such as feeling nauseated. This occurs because the body, like the psyche, is undergoing the detoxification process. Therefore, it is essential to replenish positive energy after the connections have been severed. For example, a Selenite crystal can be used to infuse the holder with positive energy. The next stage in the process of cutting the cord is to consider the role of forgiveness. This is significant because if the holder is willing to forgive themselves and others, the negative energy will not take root too deeply. This is typically what aids practitioners who confront negative cords. Additionally, it is necessary to purge the crystals after all of this labor. Cutting cables can be efficient and can be done whenever necessary, but it is still a laborious task that often requires a great deal of time and energy. It is necessary to wash one's hands and to clear and purify the stones in order to purify previously used crystals. Selenite is an excellent option because it is one of the few crystals that purifies other stones and does not require cleaning. For instance, if black kyanite is placed on selenite, selenite will purify and recharge the black kyanite.

Writing in a journal is another method for severing energetic ties. Reexamining the causes of negative energy, the amount of it, and the situations in which a person receives it is facilitated by writing things down. Occasionally, it is the holder's own negative energy that must be addressed, not negative energy from outside sources. To gain a clear view of their energy field, the holder should record the items they should release. This could consist of a variety of objects, including items from the past. This type of reflection is beneficial to one's self-awareness. Recognizing one's own faults and being able to do something about them is the essence of healing therapy. After everything has been written down, the paper should be pleated and placed beneath the black tourmaline and rose quartz. Rose quartz is the stone of forgiveness and affection, while black tourmaline encourages release.

In addition to the previously mentioned crystals selenite and black kyanite, amethyst is an effective stone for cutting cords, as it helps to release the energy affixed to the holder's third eye. After cleansing and programming the amethyst, it should be placed on the holder's third eye, causing chaotic alterations on the surface. After this disorder becomes apparent, the holder must go through the motions of physically removing the cables from their mind. Amethyst should be used to pinpoint and sever the cords as they are pulled from the holder's consciousness. When a cord is severed, it should be pictured as if it were connected into higher frequencies. Repeat the procedure until all negative cords have been severed.

Utilizing Protection Stones on a Daily Basis

Numerous crystals have protective properties and can be utilized in a variety of settings. For example, the crystals can be situated in all four corners of the holder's residence. This is a straightforward method for creating a tranquil environment in the home. Crystals can also be used for tension reduction and anxiety suppression. There are numerous types of stones with a vast array of properties that can aid in almost every aspect of life. However, the effectiveness of the protection stone is contingent on the holder's intent and specific objective.

If the purpose of the crystal is to protect fragile relationships, certain stones can be incorporated into daily life to keep individuals on course. The primary reason people seek out crystals is referred to as general positivity. The most recommended stones for protection, however, are clear quartz, amethyst, black tourmaline, and selenite. The first stone used to cleanse energies is pure quartz. Amethyst, the second crystal mentioned, is one that dispels negative energies. Black tourmaline, the third gemstone, can be used to attract even more positive energy.

Last but not least is the selenite crystal, which is an incredibly potent piece of home decor. Selenite is rumored to be capable of producing a highly positive environment. Selenite amplifies the positive energy that is already present, and it acts as a protector for all who reside nearby.

Crystals for protection can be placed under a person's pillow to ward off nightmares and facilitate restful sleep. Jade and kyanite, for instance, are the stones to use if a person wishes to remember a dream after awakening. The protection stones can be placed in vehicles to rid them of negative energy and alleviate tension or anger while driving. Amber and obsidian, turquoise and garnet, and even amethyst may be utilized for this purpose. These stones also alleviate motion nausea. If a person spends a great deal of time in front of a computer, the protection stone can be placed next to the computer to create electromagnetic pollution and protect the holder.

Crystals such as sodalite and hematite are useful for cleaning and maintaining the optimal quantity of energy for an individual in a home or office. Additionally, protection stones are not exclusively used for humans. They can also be beneficial for canines. The crystals can be placed near the pet's sleeping area or on its collar. Some stones that can be used for pets include lithium quartz, which can alleviate melancholy in pets, and dalmatian jasper, which can treat digestive issues in pets. Stones with protective properties can be used singly or in combination. Combining various crystals increases their potency. In combination, stones such as black obsidian, jasper, amethyst, jet stone, tourmaline quartz, black tourmaline, fire agate, and smokey quartz can shield the holder from negative energy and provide powerful psychic protection. It is said that crystal combinations can shield an individual from electromagnetic pollution and prevent daily judgment impairment. This allows the holder to fine-tune their psychic abilities and develop their true potential.

Developing a Defense Shield

When it comes to constructing a defense shield, there are no specific guidelines. Due to the fact that crystals function differently for each individual, each holder will have unique needs and, eventually, goals. Those who are unprepared for the true power of black obsidian rock may experience depression or lethargy. Therefore, it is not advised to use obsidian unless powerful protection is required.

Nonetheless, some crystals can be used for daily energy protection, which has no lasting effects. Whether the recipient is a teacher or a lightworker, a tourmaline pendant is an ideal gift. It is a practical method to create a protective barrier while performing daily tasks without consciously focusing on it.

Some healers assert that a protective shield can be generated by connecting the pendant with the divine energy of the Archangel Michael's spirit. Sugilite is the second crystal that can be used to erect a protection shield. This crystal reflects light and generates a spectrum of violet hues that indicate the level of protection. The first hue is a pale lilac followed by a dark magenta. The crystal transforms into a white magenta hue when moist. Sugilite is a stone used to align and regulate the crown and third eye chakras. It also serves to balance the third eye, but in order to activate it, one must imagine a shield surrounding one's environment.

Saturn Resides In The Root Chakra.

A farmer awakens to find his field overgrown with weeds, harvests scattered about, and a broken fence. After a long, hot day of back-breaking labor and tedious duties, he looks out at a storage shed filled with harvested crops, a pristine fence, and a well-kept pasture with satisfaction. Because the fruits of his labor reside in front of him as a symbol of his efficacy, consistency, concentration, and sound methods, he exudes a profound sense of self-assurance.

This is Saturn's vitality in action.

The Root Chakra is the foundation, the anchor, the origin, and our connection to death and Mother Earth. Saturn represents foundation, stability, structure, endurance, and tenacity. This energy center is the foundation of our complete being, and it is through this sphere that we materialize our essence.

Our Spirit affirms its connection to the Earth through Saturn, fostering a sense of stability and security in our foundation and purpose.

Saturn is indifferent to our desires, aspirations, dreams, and emotions. Saturn does not care what we are attempting to do, what we claim to be doing, or what we believe we are doing.

Saturn is concerned about past actions. The actual manifestation of our efforts. What do the data indicate, at the end of the day? How much cash was totaled? What was cultivated? What is the objectively manifested result of our efforts?

The glyph for Saturn is a combination of a cross and a crescent with a crescent below. The symbol represents a combination of self-consciousness and sub-consciousness in which the superconscious is absent and reason, the defining characteristic of the self-conscious plane, reigns supreme.

This symbol reveals a great deal about the Saturnian character: Saturn's success results from sound reasoning and the subordination of transient appetites and inclinations to the ego's will. We fail to effectively implement our ideas in the physical world due to an exploitation of our reasoning abilities or a lack of control over our subconscious.

Saturn is the planet of materialism, the physical universe, and Matter itself. Saturnian energy is prudent, self-controlled, security-focused, and pragmatic. Saturn is sluggish, methodical, patient, and plodding. Saturn is aware that consistency over time, regardless of how monotonous and tiresome, is what leads to success.

It is enjoyable to fantasize and daydream, but we must eventually take action to make our aspirations a reality. Saturn is the ultimate will-concentrator because our success is measured in objective, tangible terms. Saturn in our first Chakra anchors our Soul into this incarnation, and it is through incarnation that our Spirit is manifested into Matter. Saturn symbolizes the stability where life force is exchanged and replenished. Thus, Saturn's function is the cultivation of self-discipline and self-respect.

Saturn governs structures and influences the skeletal system on a cellular level. Saturn governs planning, organization, hierarchy, and chain of command. Structures are the means by which ideas and aspirations become manifested realities. Saturn rules the precautions we take to ensure the successful completion of any task or endeavor. Saturn is restrictive and unyielding. What works is implemented, and what does not, regardless of how cherished it may be, must be abandoned. Saturn governs our work ethic and our capacity to prioritize our goals over our anxieties, laziness, and emotions. Because of this, it also symbolizes the development of faith in one's destiny, which does not result from fantasizing, wishing, or expecting, but rather from effective, consistent, and concerted effort, even in the face of adversity.

Saturn's activation typically indicates that we are being evaluated. Saturn reveals the areas of our lives in which we have been slothful, irresponsible, idealistic, or ignorant, and through severe lessons compels us to strengthen these areas. Saturn transits can be some of the most joyless and dreary times; paradoxically, Saturn is the planet of faith because of this suffering! A genuinely challenging Saturn transit can break your spirit and shatter your fondest aspirations. However, he does so to expose your weaknesses and give you the chance to demonstrate your fortitude and resilience.

Saturn is the ultimate "reality-check" You may believe that you are God's gift to humanity, but a solid slap from Saturn will cure you of your arrogance and delusions. This wake-up call can motivate you to work harder so that you can achieve your full potential. If we accept the challenges Saturn forces upon us, we will eventually accomplish far more than we would have without these teachings, because we will have strengthened and improved ourselves.

If we fail to integrate Saturn's energy, we lose our bearings and become disoriented. Life becomes meaningless and void. We fall into cynicism and despondency. Embracing Saturnian energy in its entirety may not be the most thrilling or joyful experience, but it is unquestionably the basis of genuine fulfillment. Some of the most significant achievements in our lives, such as career and educational milestones, require many years to attain. Joy and enjoyment are essential components of life, but they cannot propel us to our objectives on their own. We achieve our objectives by adhering to routines, regardless of how monotonous or restrictive they may be. We achieve our objectives when we can prioritize, organize, and complete what we begin. When we apply consistent effort toward a single objective, we may not feel like dancing in the streets, but we achieve the satisfaction that comes from self-awareness and self-respect, which is a much deeper and more enduring form of happiness.

Fourth Chapter: Svadhisthana Invocations and Affirmations

Do you wish to attract favorable modifications into your life? Consider then utilizing mantras and affirmations. By focusing your mind and opening your heart, you can use these potent tools to manifest the reality you seek.

Mantras and affirmations are two potent instruments for manifesting your desires in life. If used correctly, these potent instruments can be very effective and bring about the changes you desire in your life.

Mantras are a series of repeated words or noises that have significance. These terms are frequently derived from an ancient language and have been used by believers for centuries. They are typically spoken aloud but can also be spoken quietly.

Affirmations are positive statements you make about yourself, a situation, or an outcome. Typically, an affirmation is written down and repeated until it becomes ingrained in the subconscious.

This chapter will examine the effectiveness of mantras and affirmations, as well as their function in manifestation. It will also cover selecting and employing effective affirmations in daily life.

Invocations and Affirmations

People who believe in mantras have used them for centuries because they have been repeatedly proven effective. Mantras have a similar influence on the mind as hypnosis or meditation. When you repeat a mantra, its meaning becomes ingrained in your subconscious mind and eventually influences how you think and feel about various aspects of life.

Affirmations have a similar effect as mantras. When you repeat an affirmation, it becomes ingrained in your subconscious and alters your thoughts and feelings. It is particularly effective to combine affirmations with visualizations or even a period of silent meditation.

Utilizing mantras and affirmations to manifest one's desires in life. You can use them to alter your perspective, attract wealth, enhance your relationships, restore your body, etc. The limit is the heavens.

Mantras and affirmations for Svadhisthana can improve your mood and help you manage tension more effectively. In addition, they have a calming effect on emotional imbalances such as anxiety and depression. Collectively, these techniques provide a potent instrument for empowering oneself and living an energetically balanced existence.

Here are some of the most significant advantages of using Svadhisthana mantras and affirmations:

Increased inventiveness.

More vitality and drive.

Greater mental clarity.

A more tranquil psyche and decreased stress levels.

Improved concentration and focus.

A general sense of wellbeing.

When you use mantras and affirmations to balance your chakras, you can anticipate life-wide improvement. The full potential of your energy centers is unlocked by clearing and energizing your body.

Affirmations for the Sacral Chakra, Part 1

Choosing affirmations that resonate with you personally is essential when working with them. The more connected you feel to your affirmations and how they make you feel, the more effective they will be in assisting you manifest what you wish to manifest in your life.

Here are some examples of affirmations that can be used for sacral chakra work:

I am open to new experiences and opportunities.

I welcome prosperity and abundance into my existence.

I let go of all anxiety and skepticism.

I express my limitless creativity in everything I do.

I am confident and at ease in my own environment.
I adore and accept myself exactly as I am.
I am deserving of affection, esteem, and contentment.
My relationships are wholesome, sustaining, and satisfying.

Here are some examples to help you get started. You are welcome to modify them or develop your own. Remember that it is crucial to choose affirmations that resonate with you personally.

This section examines how to formulate your own affirmations for the sacral chakra.

How to Create Your Sacral Chakra Affirmations

To write affirmations for the sacral chakra, you must contemplate the qualities governed by this energy center. These include, among others, creativity, passion, pleasure, and intuition. Create a brief statement or phrase that encapsulates each idea and expresses how you want to feel.

When crafting affirmations, it is also essential to have a purpose in mind. You might begin with a simple statement such as "I am creative" or "I am filled with passion." Use these as the basis for more particular claims, such as "My creative energy flows freely at all times" or "I am passionate about embracing my unique voice and style." Consider why you want to strengthen your sacral chakra, what specific benefits you expect to attain, and how you want to feel as a result of using these techniques.

Consider the areas of your life in which you'd like to experience more creativity and passion; this will help you get started with your sacral chakra affirmations. For instance, do you need assistance discovering new inspiration for your writing or artistic endeavors? Where in your personal life would you like to see more pleasure and spontaneity? Do you wish to establish a stronger connection with your intuition and develop faith in the incoming guidance? By having a clear intention, you can construct affirmations that will assist you in achieving your specific objectives.

Guidelines for Formulating Unique Affirmations

There are numerous methods to formulate affirmations that encourage authenticity and open communication. Additionally, it is beneficial to concentrate on the qualities or characteristics you venerate most in yourself and others. For example, if you value confidence and creativity, you might create an affirmation such as "I am a naturally confident person who overcomes obstacles with ease." In order for your affirmations to emanate from a genuine place of self-acceptance, it is vital that you ruminate on these qualities as you write them.

Specificity is another essential component of engaging affirmations. While it may seem sufficient to simply state, "I am a kind and compassionate person," delving deeper into this concept can help you construct more meaningful phrases that resonate more strongly with you. Consider concentrating on actions that demonstrate kindness, such as demonstrating compassion for others, offering advice without judgment, and assisting loved ones in need. These specific statements serve as reminders that you are living in accordance with your values and beliefs.

Lastly, formulate your affirmations in a way that feels intuitive to you. While certain forms of structured meditation emphasize the repetition of specific phrases throughout the day, a more natural approach to affirmations can also be beneficial. Instead of compelling yourself to adhere to a rigid schedule, keep your affirmations in mind throughout the day and allow them to arise naturally.

Mantras for the Sacral Chakra, Part 2

In addition to crafting affirmations for the sacral chakra, it is also advantageous to consistently employ mantras. These Sanskrit words can be repeated audibly or internally, with a focus on a single syllable that is intended to resonate with the energy of this chakra. The following mantras can be used to support the sacral chakra as you open yourself to new inspiration, embrace your inherent creativity, and develop a more passionate outlook on life.

Vam Mantra for Svadhisthana Chakra

The first mantra associated with the sacral chakra is "vam." This word is pronounced "vahm" and means "I"; therefore, it is the ideal mantra for fostering self-acceptance and inner fortitude. This mantra can be repeated whenever you feel disconnected from yourself, and it is particularly effective when chanted with an emphasis on the abdomen and lower back.

The vam mantra is intended to stimulate and balance the sacral chakra. The Sanskrit word "vam" also means "water" and represents the fluid, creative energy of this chakra. By regularly reiterating this mantra, we facilitate the flow of creative energy in our lives. As a result, our intimate relationships flourish and our creative endeavors become more effortless. Today, chant the vam mantra for yourself and observe the changes in your life.

"Om Mani Padme Hum" is the mantra of the Sacral Chakra.

The mantra for the second sacral chakra is "om mani padme hum." This phrase is pronounced "oh-muh-nee-pahd-may-hoom," which translates to "jewel in the lotus." This mantra is commonly used as a meditation aid and is associated with Buddhist tradition. By concentrating on the energy of this mantra, we activate our sacral chakra and strengthen our connection to our innate creativity.

It is also said that this mantra represents the path to spiritual development. By reiterating this mantra, we constantly remind ourselves that we are on the path to enlightenment. The lotus flower in this mantra represents our capacity for growth and transformation, whereas the jewel represents the insight we can attain through this process.

Mantra for Svadhisthana Chakra: "Muladhara"

The mantra for the third sacral chakra is "Muladhara." This term is pronounced "moo-lah-dah-rah," and it means "root support." This mantra is designed to help us ground and balance our energy, making it the ideal mantra for those who experience an unbalanced sacral chakra.

This mantra can be repeated whenever you feel uncentered, scattered, or exhausted. By intentionally repeating this mantra, you realign your energy and restore your equilibrium. It is also believed that the word "Muladhara" represents the four extremities of the Earth, reminding us that the ground supports our feet.

Namo Mantra

The mantra for the fourth sacral chakra is "namo." This word, pronounced "nah-moh," means "bow to the divine within me." This mantra is meant to help us communicate with our inner wisdom, and it can be repeated whenever we need guidance or support in our lives.

This mantra serves as a reminder that we all have access to divine guidance, which we can access by turning inward. The word "namo" also signifies humility, reminding us that we all share the same divine energy. You will find that repeating this mantra helps to open your mind and heart, allowing you to embrace the universe's wisdom.

So Hum Mantra

The mantra for the fifth sacral chakra is "so hum." These words are pronounced "soh-hoom," and they mean "I am." This mantra serves as a reminder that we are all connected to the divine and comprised of the same energy as the cosmos. It can be repeated whenever you seek to connect with your inner wisdom or wish to access the divine energy that surrounds us.

This mantra is also believed to be the sound of the universe and is frequently used in meditation. By repeating this mantra, we are able to silence our minds and connect with the inner peace and tranquility. This mantra can also be used to connect with the essence of all life, serving as a reminder that we are a part of something much larger than ourselves.

Maha Mrityunjaya Mantra

The mantra for the sixth sacral chakra is the "maha mrityunjaya mantra." This is pronounced "muh-huh-muh-ree-toon-jah-yuh," and it means "great death conqueror." This mantra can be used to help us surmount fear and anxiety, and it is frequently recommended to those who are navigating challenging life transitions. It is believed to contain the power of transformation and to assist us in releasing old patterns and modes of being that no longer serve us.

This mantra is also said to symbolize the cycle of life and mortality, serving as a reminder that change is an unavoidable aspect of existence. As we purposefully repeat this mantra, we release the dread and anxiety that are holding us back. The word "mahamrityunjaya" also represents the three sacred aspects, reminding us that we are always supported by a higher power. Your existence regains its strength and equilibrium as you repeat this mantra.

Om Namah Shivaya Mantra

"Om namah Shivaya" is the mantra of the seventh sacral chakra. It is pronounced "ohm nah-muh-shee-vuh-yuh" and signifies "I bow to Shiva." This mantra serves as a reminder that we are all connected to the divine and comprised of the same energy as the cosmos. It can be repeated whenever you seek to connect with your inner wisdom or wish to access the divine energy that surrounds us.

How to Use These Mantras

Now that you are familiar with some of the most popular mantras for the sacral chakra, here are some guidelines for using them effectively:

Find a peaceful location where you can unwind and concentrate on your mantra. This area should ideally be as still and quiet as feasible.

Before beginning, take a few deep breaths to help soothe your mind and relax your body.

Focus solely on your mantra and banish all other notions from your mind.

Intentionally repeat your mantra slowly and distinctly.

Observe how your mantra makes you feel after you've given it time to settle in.

Be patient with yourself, and if your mind wanders during meditation, do not fret. Simply return your focus to your mantra as soon as you realize it has wandered.

If possible, practice this technique daily and, as you feel ready, add additional affirmations.

After only a few weeks of practice, you should begin to perceive the benefits of these mantras. They can assist you in relieving stress, establishing a connection with the divine, and finding more serenity in your daily life. You may find that, with time and practice, these mantras become an integral part of your identity.

The sacral chakra is located close to the sacrum at the base of the spine and is related to creativity, vitality, passion, pleasure, and sexuality. Using the appropriate affirmations and mantras for the sacral chakra, you can balance this energy center and bring more harmony into your life. Observe how these daily mantras and affirmations make you feel, and you will be astonished by the positive changes you experience.

Whether you are seeking to relax and connect with your inner wisdom or bring more healing energy into your life, these mantras are an excellent starting point. For the greatest results, remember to be patient with yourself and to practice regularly. You should observe a difference in your life with time and dedication.

Solar Plexus Pranayama And Yoga

What Is Pranayama?

Pranayama is the fourth limb of yoga and its literal translation is "control of air" or "extension of breath." It literally translates to "breath control." It is a potent form of meditation that can aid in calming the mind, healing the body, and achieving many other benefits. Pranayama aims to connect the breath to the emotional centers of the body. When combined, these two can combat physical effects such as depression and tension.

Pranayama is predicated on the idea that, similar to electricity, prana (the Sanskrit term for "energy") flows through the body. The passage of prana can be obstructed by improper posture, anxiety, or fatigue. Although it is difficult to alter one's circumstances, a little bit of effort can transform one's existence.

The prana, or life force, is mobilized and regulated by this yogic technique. Traditionally, Pranayama is used to balance the mind and body. The breathing techniques used in this practice can assist in calming an overactive mind and body, clearing the mind, reducing anxiety, lowering blood pressure, and relieving stress and muscle tension. There are numerous pranayama techniques that anyone, regardless of age or gender, can practice.

Why Pranayama Matters

Pranayama is the most significant aspect of yoga and is regarded as an essential technique. There is a reason why yoga postures are performed backward, upside down, and in odd positions. This is due to the fact that they all stimulate various energy centers in the body.

Additionally, being immersed in zero gravity (such as lying down) can help you relax, sleep, and restore your body. In conjunction with yoga postures and meditation, yogic breathing techniques grant us access to the power of our brain waves and subconscious mind, thereby facilitating the desired changes. This skill allows us to remain grounded and connected to our surroundings. It's also the reason we sleep when we're exhausted or anxious.

Pranayama is a crucial component of yoga because it is one of the techniques used to control the respiration. Pranayama is one of the four main components of yoga (along with asana, pratyahara, and Dharana) that helps you achieve inner calm.

Pranayama is one of the most effective techniques for improving physical and mental health through breathwork. It is a potent tool that can help you relax and quiet your consciousness. Pranayama effectively reduces tension and protects against stress-related disorders and diseases because it profoundly affects both the mind and body by altering brainwave patterns via slowed breathing.

When experiencing tension or anxiety, you breathe irregularly and shallowly. You are also more likely to contract infectious diseases if your immune system is compromised. Therefore, pranayama is essential for overall health and fitness.

Bhramari Pranayama for Your Manipura

The Bhramari Pranayama, also known as "bumblebee breath," is one of the most effective forms of breathwork for the Manipura chakra. This is an excellent form of breathwork that will aid in the healing of your mind, and it also has a calming influence on your nervous system. You will emit a sound resembling that of a bumblebee, a gentle humming sound that causes vibrations to travel throughout your entire body. These vibrations facilitate the transition of your nervous system to the parasympathetic system, which your body employs to rest and digest. Additionally, it impacts the vagus nerve.

Why is the vagus nerve important? Because it is responsible for initiating the processes that allow for rest and digestion. In other terms, it is directly connected to the solar plexus chakra's inner fire. This nerve travels from the brain stem, down the neck, and into the abdomen. In addition, it provides the pathway for hormones to travel along the brain-gut axis. The brain-gut axis is the reason you can feel mentally at ease with yourself, as you are aware. In fact, your digestion dictates your mood, which is why you must be selective about the foods you consume. About 95% of your body's serotonin, a neurotransmitter that assists with neural functions and mood stabilization, is produced in your intestines.

You can use either higher or lower tones when meditating using this form of pranayama. Since you're working on the solar plexus chakra, it's beneficial to use both tones, as it's near to the heart chakra, which is the energy center that sits in the middle of all the others. Additionally, it is prudent to attempt to chant in the key of E. Why E? Due to the fact that this tone corresponds precisely to the solar plexus chakra, you will direct all of the energy generated by the breath-work to this specific energy center. You can also target other energy centers with this type of pranayama if you so choose. It's a matter of modifying the tone and focusing on the energy center in question, but since this book is all about the solar plexus, we'll do so instead.

How to Breathe Like a Bumblebee

Find a place where you won't be disturbed or distracted for the next fifteen minutes. Ensure that you are wearing loose, comfortable clothing that allows you to breathe freely.

Find a comfortable position to recline. You can position both hands on your lap or plug your ears with your index fingers while pointing your elbows out to the sides.

As you settle in and become comfortable, take three thorough inhales and exhales through your nostrils.

Focus your awareness on the solar plexus chakra. If desired, you can visualize it.

As you exhale, press down on the cartilage of your ears to block them and produce a buzzing sound, similar to that of a bee.

Imagine that as you breathe in, bright yellow energy enters the solar plexus chakra, and as you breathe out, the solar plexus chakra becomes more radiant and attractive.

Repeat this pattern six to seven times (1 repetition consists of an inhale and an expiration).

You may take a respite, then continue breathing in this manner for the next five minutes or until you feel you have completed sufficient work for the session.

What Is Yoga?

Yoga is an ancient practice with origins in India that date back more than 5,000 years. It is founded on the concept of connecting with one's inner self. Those who practice yoga believe that breathing and poses, or "asanas," unify all aspects of the mind and body. Yoga practice induces a tranquil and more relaxed state. Yoga is not only a form of exercise, but also a way of life.

Yoga is a discipline that can help you achieve balance in your life through meditation and breathwork. There is empirical evidence that yoga reduces tension, anxiety, and depression. It can also be an effective method for maintaining flexibility and engaging muscle groups for strength training. There are numerous types of yoga suitable for everyone, from beginners to advanced practitioners.

The Benefits of Yoga for the Solar Plexus Chakra

The solar plexus chakra governs your material relationships and your passions. The sense of well-being you will attain through yoga practice can assist you in discovering your genuine passions. Your solar plexus chakra governs your ability to feel, think, and act from a place of intuition and inspiration rather than dread, confusion, and hesitation by nourishing your body with the nutrients it requires to feel healthy, happy, and fit.

Yoga is also a practice that enables us to recognize our true needs in life. In yoga, we are not dependent on others for our requirements, but rather on ourselves. Only you can fulfill your needs in a manner that will make you genuinely happy. Yoga can equip you with the skills necessary to meet your own requirements.

Yoga's physical benefits may also benefit the solar plexus chakra. This chakra controls how the body and mind react to tension and anxiety, or their absence. The various yoga poses alleviate stress and anxiety not only on a mental but also a physical level by making you more flexible and stronger on both the mental and physical levels, allowing you to manage stressful situations with less pain and discomfort. Numerous individuals discover that as their health and fitness improve, their outlook on life improves as well. Once we learn how to manage tension and anxiety in our daily lives, according to yogic philosophy, we become more balanced and less susceptible to illness.

Additionally, yoga is an ancient healing practice that extends back thousands of years before Western medicine. Yoga is now the fastest-growing form of alternative medicine in the United States, surpassing traditional medicines such as herbal remedies and doctor visits by a significant margin. Yoga has been so beneficial because it teaches you how to control your thoughts and emotions by adapting your behavior, resulting in improved health and greater tranquility.

Blue

One of the most popular colors to date is blue; the color of sea, sky, freshness and freedom. In fact, it is known as the color most used for company logos. It is commonly associated with trust, loyalty, inspiration, innovativeness, sincerity and communication. Let us take a deeper look at this cool color.

Blue: The Color of Communication and Community

This color is often used as a symbol of water, ice or other things that are moist or cold. This is quite the opposite of what red showed us earlier. While red is more hot, dry, and associated with the masculine archetype; blue is very feminine with the exception of being the color for baby boys (pink being for baby girls). It is feminine since blue's qualities are very family or community oriented.

Blue is the color of the ocean that connects all the fish and the color of the sky/air that we are all surrounded by. In the United States, the Democratic Party, which is symbolized by blue has very matriarchal viewpoint while the Republican Party has more patriarchal views (being symbolized with red).

Water is often a symbol for the fluidity of our emotions to add to feminine archetype of blue. Like the moon changes the tides of the ocean during its monthly cycle, a female body also has its own monthly cycle which can affect their emotions.

Looking at the sea or a blue colored object or being in an environment adorned with blue stimulates calmness and triggers the release of different hormones in your body that exude tranquility, serenity and calmness. That said, not every hue of blue has a sedative or serene effect. Bright or electric blues have a dramatic and dynamic effect.

An excess of blue can bring about feelings of negativity, melancholy, sadness, self-centeredness and self-righteousness whereas too little of it brings about depression, unreliability, timidity, stubbornness and suspicion.

Blue also symbolizes piety, friendliness and sincerity. Blue in most of cultures symbolizes peace, religious beliefs and the subconscious. It is also the color of the throat chakra.

Blue: Color of Fifth Chakra

The throat chakra, aka 'Vishuddha' in Sanskrit, means 'extremely pure' and is the fifth chakra of the lot. It is located in your throat and governs your ability to speak, express yourself, listen and engage with people. It is also related to your thyroid and parathyroid glands, mouth and throat.

When it is balanced, it provides relief against headaches, fevers, earaches, migraines, sore throat, eyestrain and keeps your blood pressure stable. Blue is the color of the throat chakra and it is important to keep it in balance to keep your throat chakra active.

When the throat chakra is blocked, you experience great difficulty in communicating with others, expressing yourself and suffer from headaches, pain in shoulders and neck, cough and cold as well as hearing and thyroid related issues. In addition, you are unable to connect to your spiritual and intuitive side and find a clearer direction in life.

An active and balanced throat chakra helps you avoid all these problems and live a harmonious life. To achieve that, use blue colored gemstones, wear blue clothes often and visualize blue light entering and filling your throat chakra daily for 10 minutes. While you enjoy the benefits of blue in your life, also learn other interpretations of this color.

Different Interpretations of Blue

- Blue symbolizes mourning and pain in Iran and is often worn by the relatives of a deceased person.
- In the Western countries, brides have a tradition of carrying something blue with them on their wedding day as it symbolizes love.
- The phrases 'getting the blues' and 'feeling blue' refers to depression and sadness.
- The commonly used phrase 'out of the blue' is used to refer to the occurrence of an unexpected event.

- 'True blue' is another commonly used expression that signifies a trustworthy and faithful person.
- A blue colored ribbon symbolizes first prize or winner.

Blue definitely is a color with many meanings and one, which can certainly add calmness and serenity to your life. Now let us take a closer look at indigo.

Chapter 9: How to Care for Your Third Eye

The thing about opening your third eye, as you've probably deduced from some of the stories from the previous chapter, is that it's a very powerful experience that you absolutely need to make sure you're prepared for. Because it's so intense and scary, you must ensure that you take care of your third eye. This chapter will explain some practices you can use to care for this purpose.

How to Handle Overactivity

Most people are interested in opening their third eye without being aware that you can do so to an extent where it's overactive. One of the leading causes of overactivity in this energy center is not having support or balance from the others. Have you ever had a little too much coffee when you're extremely tired? It feels like you have all this energy, but you cannot channel it to any specific thing. That's exactly what it's like when you open your third eye chakra without doing energy work on the lower chakras first. It's absolutely essential, again, to start from the root and work your way up to the crown.

An overactive Ajna can cause nausea, insomnia, sinus problems, and sleep issues. Other non-physical problems are paranoia, mental fog, depression, anxiety, issues with concentration, and even hallucinations.

If you are having problems with this chakra, it could be a sign that you're not willing to take a deep look at yourself and face the fears you have continued to ignore for years. When you're unwilling or unable to face the truth about who you are, you can't reason clearly, and you find your mind cluttered with doubt and worries about being criticized or judged by others. When you are plagued by overactivity in this energy center, you experience bitterness, anger, jealousy, and other negative emotions that set you many steps back along your path of spiritual development and healing.

Healing Your Ajna

You can do so many things to help your third eye chakra heal. Whatever method you decide to use, it's important to consider your personality and what would work best for your schedule. So, think of the following as suggestions that you can tweak as needed to help you heal your third eye. When you put them into practice, you will experience real results. Above everything else, you must bring mindfulness into whatever you do. The fact that you already want to take steps to heal yourself says you are well on the way to healing and finding balance.

Consider your diet. You must ensure you nourish your body with the right foods to help your third eye chakra find balance. There is a connection between your physical body and your energy body. Whatever you do with one affects the other. This is why eating the right foods for your third eye is essential. You should include purple cabbage, blueberries, plums, and eggplants in your diet. Eating natural purple foods can help your third eye chakra balance itself out. Also, foods with a lot of omega-3 fatty acids can help it heal. Go for edamame, chia seeds, algae, seaweed, vegetables, trout, mackerel, shrimp, and salmon. You can also add some chocolate to your diet, but make sure it's dark. The darker, the better. You'll find it helps you clear your mind and relax.

Start doing more therapeutic activities. Creativity and imagination are connected to the third eye chakra. When you do more therapeutic creative exercises like drawing, painting, writing, singing, and so on, you will cause your third eye chakra to find balance. Other therapeutic activities include alternate nostril breathing and other meditation forms so you can go into deeper levels of consciousness.

Use energy healing to your advantage. Reiki is an excellent way to bring balance to all your energy centers. It's about channeling energy into your body using touch. You could also work with sound therapy or aromatherapy. Sound therapy, in particular, is very effective because of the vibrational frequencies produced by the music you listen to, which affects your third eye chakra. For aromatherapy, all you need are the essential oils we've already discussed.

Move more. When you make exercise a regular practice in your day-to-day life, you will bring balance to your body. Yoga, in particular, is very great for healing your energy centers. The best poses to help your third eye find balance are the eagle pose, tree pose, forward bends, shoulder stands, child's pose, plow pose, lotus pose, bridge, and downward dog.

Work with the magic of stones. You can wear the following jewelry or simply hold them in your hands while meditating: purple fluorite, labradorite, opal, moonstone, quartz, amethyst, and lapis lazuli.

Use guided meditations. There are so many medications out there that you can use to heal your third eye chakra. Some of these are paid-for services offered by professional chakra healers, while others are free on the Internet. A simple search on YouTube will bring you a lot of results, so you can choose the one that is most viewed as effective. Before you begin guided meditation, ensure you will not be distracted. If you don't live on your own, make sure you inform the people who live with you that they need to give you some time to yourself and be as quiet as they can be. Wear comfortable and loose clothing and keep an open mind. Never go into any guided meditation session with expectations. Simply flow with it. Also, if you do these sessions more than once, don't think it will be like the last time. You may experience something right away, but this does not always happen. It doesn't matter. What matters is that you are doing the work to bring your third eye back into balance.

Use the skull's shining breath. This pranayama technique is not just for opening your third eye but also for bringing it into balance. If you notice you're starting to have adverse effects from opening your third eye, you should practice this breathing technique daily. The more you do this exercise, the better you'll be able to handle all the psychic phenomena happening in your life, and the less intense and scary it'll be for you.

Practice Trataka. This form of meditation requires you to gaze at a candle flame for one to three minutes without blinking. When you have finished gazing at the flame, close your eyes. You should see an afterimage of the candle's flame still. Keep your attention on the afterimage for a few minutes until it's gone. Open your eyes and take a look at the flame again. Repeat the process.

Reduce your exposure to blue light. Blue light exposure comes from using your mobile phone, television, and other screens that cause melatonin to be secreted at a less than optimal level from your pineal gland. Invest in blue-light-blocking glasses with orange lenses so you can use them in the evenings with your screens. There are also apps available on Android, Windows, and Apple operating systems that help you block blue light by adjusting the temperature of the color on your screen. These apps are usually free, so you can download them and use them immediately.

Take vitamin B12 and vitamin K2. B12 is great for helping you convert the melatonin secreted by the pineal gland. Opt for the sublingual form of this supplement. To help you heal and decalcify your pineal gland, you can take vitamin K2, specifically MK4 and MK7. They'll help remove all the calcium from your soft tissues, and they work wonderfully well with vitamin A, retinol, and vitamin D3. You need 600 mcg each day.

Cut out vegetable oil, flour, and sugar from your diet. Most, if not all, packaged foods have these ingredients in them, and they are unhelpful for your gut microbiome. They can also cause inflammation in your body.

Deal with your leaky gut. Intestinal permeability can cause inflammation in the body and in the gut-brain axis. See a medical professional to discuss what you can do to heal your leaky intestinal gut. This process will help you decalcify your pineal gland and, consequently, help your third eye be healthier.

Go to bed in complete darkness. As evening approaches, it gets darker, which helps your melatonin release cycle along. This cycle takes 4 hours. When exposed to artificial light, you have trouble with your melatonin release, and there is no balance in the secretion of melatonin to serotonin in your pineal gland.

Get some sun every day. If you're not an early riser, now is a good time to change that. Wake up early in the morning so you can look at the sun as it rises. Morning sunlight helps your circadian rhythm start up, which will help the rate of melatonin release from your pineal gland to be balanced.

Your pineal gland secretes melatonin, which regulates your circadian or sleep-wake rhythms, which are critical to lucid dreams, out-of-body projections, and psychic phenomena. When you suffer from low melatonin, your pineal gland cannot produce enough of it, disrupting your sleep cycles. Disrupted sleep cycles mean you will not get the benefits of lucid dreaming and out-of-body projections, and you won't have the added advantage of a healthy third eye.

Practice color visualization. According to yoga philosophy and third eye chakra theory, your third eye is connected to the color indigo. This is a color that is deep blue, almost purple. You should check this out on the Internet to be sure of what you should be visualizing. Close your eyes and imagine that you have a deep blue-purple glowing orb right where your third eye should be. Keep this image in your mind for at least 5 minutes.

Try sensory deprivation. Your pineal gland is very sensitive to light. So whenever possible, it's beneficial to get into complete darkness and remain there for a while. If you want to experience what it's like to be completely cut off from your 5 senses, you'll need a sensory deprivation tank or a float tank. To make use of the tank, you have to get in, and you'll be floating in the water, disconnected from all senses.

There are many benefits to be had from this practice.

As you are cut off from all sensory stimulation, including sight, sound, and gravity, you will float in the darkness, weightless, and your brain will go into a very relaxed state. You may experience visions, hallucinations, and even experience deeper levels of creativity than you've ever had. Sensory deprivation is also wonderful for helping you think precisely and improving your concentration and focus. You'll find yourself doing better at work or in school after that. This is also a great way to get rid of anxiety or stress. Also, if you're experiencing chronic pain, you will find it is a great way to relieve yourself.

Using sensory deprivation tanks can also help you feel euphoric and happy. When you're experiencing positive feelings and emotions, this naturally feeds your energy body with good energy and can remove any blocks that you may be experiencing. In other words, this is an excellent way to clear out your third eye chakra and heal it if it's out of balance as well. The trouble with float tanks is that they can be very pricey. They cost anywhere from $10,000 to $30,000. Alternatively, depending on local prices, you can go to a floatation center or spa and spend between $50 and $100 for a session. Please note that you have to take off all your jewelry and clothing before getting into the tank, and it's a good idea to take a shower before you get in. Enter the tank and close the lid or door. Then let the water help you to float. For the first 10 minutes of your session, music will play. This music is supposed to help you relax. The music will come back on when your session is about to end. If you want to make the most of your experience, you should have something to eat about 30 minutes beforehand. If you're a coffee person, please don't have any caffeine for four hours before your session. Wasting or shaving before your session is not advised because the salt in the water can cause your skin to feel irritated. If you're on your period, please reschedule your session for when it has finished.

To make this experience even more powerful, you can focus on your third eye while your eyes are shut in the tank. Chanting a mantra like OM could also help. You can also envision yourself being surrounded and engulfed by pure white light that flows through all of your chakras. Remember, every chakra needs to be balanced to work together. Just like you wouldn't build a house without first having your foundation in place, you need to ensure your root chakra, sacral chakra, and every other chakra leading up to the third eye chakra are in balance. Also, just because the third eye is the most talked-about does not mean you should ignore developing your crown chakra. Use this time in the tank to feed your energy body.

Utilize affirmatives. When used properly, affirmations can help you restore balance to the center of your forehead. They are extremely potent because you are literally expressing your thoughts through words, which then shape your reality. You can use the following affirmations to restore your chakras:

I am open and receptive to receiving guidance from within.

I nourish my spirit and my essence.

I have access to the most profound and genuine source of compassion and light within myself.

I am profoundly conscious that all is well.

I am capable and willing to pardon myself.

The past is history. I learned all the lessons I needed to from it, and then I left them there.

For me, life flows effortlessly.

I embrace myself in my current state.

I am in tune with the universe's and life's profound wisdom.

My natural state of being is tranquility.

I am intuitive by nature.

My heart and senses are always attuned to the guidance of my higher self.

I always know precisely what I need to know at any given time.

People mistakenly believe that in order to heal your chakras, you must do it on your own. However, this is not the case. There are numerous qualified professionals available who can provide the necessary guidance and help you successfully complete the process. Keep in mind that healing your third eye chakra or any other chakras is not a linear process, and there is no one-size-fits-all approach you can take. Don't attempt to make something work for you if it's not meant to; we all have very different life paths, and that's the way it's intended to be.

Always be adaptable and remain true to yourself.

Utilize Throat Chakra To Speak Your Inner Truth

The throat chakra is:

The pharynx chakra, also known as Vishuddha, is the first of the three profound chakras. It oversees the anatomical regions of the tongue, neck, mandible, parathyroid, mouth, thyroid, and larynx in the territory of the throat. Interestingly, this chakra entails higher-level correspondence. In addition, self-assurance and comprehension comprise the essence of the vishuddha chakra. The component and perception associated with the fifth chakra are hearing and space, respectively.

In addition, it involves self-expression, correspondence, opulence, and sagacity.

This is the Mother Chakra, which initiates the body's three YIN or female vitality chakras. You can use your voice to dispense torment or consideration. Moreover, it is essential to know that the voice corresponds to our objective. We will declare something, and it will come to pass. Therein lies the enigma of indication.

Genuine expression is not something that occurs naturally. There is a distinction between saying what you intend and remaining prudent or prudent. Frequently, it is easier to express what the other person wants to hear as opposed to speaking the truth. Your sincere expression may be hindered by apprehension of not being acknowledged. Furthermore, the opinions of others may inhibit your sincere verbal expression.

If you are acclimated to being agreeable, you may need to practice so that everyone can hear what you have to say. Insistences are useful for making your desires a reality. Record what you may need to communicate with others. Determine the words you wish to say to others. Rehearse the conversation in front of a mirror.

Release of the Throat Chakra

While mental and emotional disorders can manifest in a variety of physical symptoms, physical illness can also affect your chakra structure. For example, if you have laryngitis, your larynx chakra may be impacted and require purification. Therefore, certain practices must be performed to purify the pharynx chakra.

The following are some techniques for opening your larynx chakra and allowing it to speak the truth:

Sing just for yourself

Singing is one of the most effective ways to purify the vocal chakra. Consequently, engage in harmonizing. This will activate this chakra and give you the confidence to speak.

Consume a lot of water

Water will also aid in the expansion of your throat chakra. We are fortunate to have access to water here. Use it frequently to strengthen your chakra.

Engage in hip-expanding positions.

An imbalance in other chakras can specifically affect the pharynx chakra. The hips are another location where psychological weight is stored. In addition, the next time you practice profound hip-openers while performing yoga poses, pay attention to how you sense a discharge in your throat.

Imagine blue color

As blue is the color associated with this chakra, visualize a brilliant blue radiance at the base of your throat or in other areas where you are experiencing difficulty. As you inhale while visualizing the color blue, you will experience relief and agony in these areas. Exhale and feel the tension and anxiety leaving your body as you exhale.

Use of jewels

The following gemstones are used to pacify the chakra:

Sapphire Blue topaz

Lapis lazuli

Aquamarine Turquoise Yoga practices

The following yoga positions are beneficial for addressing throat imbalances:

Camel pose-Ustrasana

Bridge pose-Setu Bandhu Sarvangasa

Shoulder stand-Salamba Sarvangasana

Plow-Halasana

Claims of the pharynx chakra

Affirmation of throat chakra is another effective method utilized by many individuals to balance the throat chakra. In this technique, the individual repeats affirmations such as, "I have the right to speak the truth at all times." Other affirmations include, "I can express all of my emotions with ease" and "I am able to express my creative thoughts to anyone, whenever I choose."

As with the heart chakra, this chakra is frequently impeded by holding onto blame. In addition, cleansing your throat chakra can bring to light things that have been in the shadows for a long time. It is unfortunate that we must endure painful feelings, thoughts, and encounters before arriving at a magnificent en. Therefore, these difficulties are worthwhile if your larynx chakra aids you in speaking the truth to others. Start taking advantage of this quality and provide your general environment with the finest version of yourself. By engaging in this activity, you may experience greater happiness and delight than you anticipated or provided.

Chapter 3 Meditation Techniques Synopsis

Although there are numerous approaches to Shakra reflection, the fundamental principles remain the same. The most important of these standards is eliminating obstructive, negative, and meandering thoughts and visions and replacing them with a profound sense of core interest. This rids the brain of garbage and prepares it for a higher level of astion.

Strategies

Negative thoughts, such as those of noisy neighbors, bossy coworkers, a traffic ticket, and undesirable sram, are said to contribute to the "sontaminating" of the brain, and closing them out i accounts for the "rurifying" of the pyche so that it can focus on deeper, more significant ideas.

A few specialists even block out all tangible information – no sights, no sounds, and nothing to touch – in an effort to isolate themselves from the surrounding din. If this is your goal, you may now concentrate on a profound, significant thought. As you continue with this activity, you will become more aware of your surroundings.

In the event that you find the pondering positions you see on television incapacitating those with unimaginably curved backs and excruciating-appearing deformities, you need not be concerned. The rule in this instance is to be in a position conducive to concentration. This may occur while seated, standing, resting, or casually meandering.

If the position allows you to relax and concentrate, then that would be an excellent starting point. While seated or standing, the back should be erect, but not strained or tense. Different positions prohibit slouching and falling asleep.

Tight-fitting garments have a tendency to suffocate and make you feel constricted, whereas loose-fitting garments allow you to move freely.

The area where you reflect should have a calming atmosphere. It could be in your living room, bedroom, or wherever you feel most comfortable. You may need an astivity mat if you intend to tackle more difficult positions (if you feel more centered in such positions, or if the flexible performer in you is yelling for release). You may need to have the srot arranged so that it is calming to your senses.

The vast majority of people require quiet to unwind and reflect, so you may require a tranquil, secluded space far from the ringing of the telephone or the humming of the washing machine. Satisfying fragrances likely aid in this regard, so stocking up on fragrant candles is not such a bad idea either.

Friars making those monotonous noises on television are actually reciting their mantra. This is, in simple terms, a brief doctrine, a fundamental tone that, for these professionals, has a spiritualist quality.

However, it is worth noting that focusing on repetitive activities, such as breathing and murmuring, helps the expert achieve a higher state of consciousness. This guideline is of primary importance. You could also try concentrating on a specific object or thought, or even, while keeping your eyes closed, on a single sight.

An example of a routine would be naming all aspects of your body while in a reflective state and focusing your attention on that part. While performing this task, you should be mindful of any pressure on your body. Imagine rationally relieving this pressure. It functions ponders.

The Heart Chakra, The Fourth Chakra.

The Heart Chakra is situated in the center of the thorax, at heart level.

Diversity and presentation

The element of this chakra is air, and its color is green. The color green is associated with healing, acknowledging the healing power of the heart chakra and the capacity to bring wholeness to our lives, just as green is the color of rebirth in nature. It also represents equilibrium, tranquility, and peace. The chakra is represented by a lotus flower with twelve petals.

Description

The heart chakra is where the seven other chakras converge. There are three chakras below the heart, which we've already discussed, and three chakras above the heart. The heart chakra has the power to revitalize all body parts and aid in the healing and restoration of all other chakras. It is the point that can expand our energy and distribute it to all of our body's regions. In a culture where intellect and rational thought are prioritized over all other virtues, the chakra is frequently shut down. The heart chakra does not reject rational thought, but it does make room for loving and kindheartedness, authenticity, and the expression of one's genuine desires. It is the connection between the psyche and the body. According to Ilchi Lee, "life is a constant process of opening and re-opening the heart chakra." This means that as a result of life's experiences, the heart chakra can either become overly sensitive, causing an individual to feel vulnerable, or it can close down. It is a lifetime's work to nourish the heart chakra by forgiving oneself, forgiving others, learning from experience, remaining hopeful even in the face of extreme adversity, and embracing experiences and people with compassion, which is not always easy and may require conscious effort.

A person with a healthy heart chakra will experience love and compassion in their lives, be able to let go of negative experiences with relative ease, as if eliminating toxins from the body, and embrace negative emotions such as grief, sorrow, and sadness, able to grow and learn from their pain, rooted in the knowledge that it will not last forever. When functioning properly, the heart chakra will create a balance between logic and emotion, as well as between the ideal state and the actual state of affairs, enabling a person to be loving, kind, and compassionate while maintaining healthy boundaries and knowing their own limits.

What occurs when this chakra is deficient?

Our life experiences influence who we are, and for a variety of reasons, there may come a time when we become aloof, distant from intimacy, and even cynical. While the reasons for this behavior may be valid and understandable – for example, you may have been betrayed by a spouse, a partner, or a family member – continuing to harbor resentment over what has transpired will only cause you further damage. It is healthy to allow yourself time to heal your wounds after a bad breakup or loss, surrendering to the grief or anger of your situation, but it is also important to let these feelings go, or you risk imitating the actions of your perpetrator or sabotaging relationships that could otherwise be successful and nourishing for you. When your heart has been wounded, you may close off your heart chakra, becoming aloof and lacking in empathy. You may be selective about the individuals you choose to love and find it difficult to let them into your life. You may find intimacy difficult, and you may criticize the people you care about for what you perceive to be a good reason. You may have a feeling that you are unworthy and unlovable on a deep level, and you may even see confirmations of this belief in your daily life – people may constantly let you down, fail to keep their commitments or promises, and your mind will interpret this as confirmation that you deserve to be mistreated.

What occurs if this chakra becomes overactive?

When your heart chakra is overactive, and quite possibly overcompensating for a blockage in one of your lower chakras, you may find yourself becoming overly attached to others and emotionally vulnerable. Depending on who you've interacted with or what you've been contemplating, you may experience the full continuum of emotions in a single day. You may tell yourself, for instance, that you will only adore a particular person if they fulfill one of your requirements. You may be a person who attempts to satisfy others in order to feel accepted. You may find yourself in a relationship where you carry all the emotional baggage; for instance, you may be the one who constantly pursues reconciliation or is the first to say 'sorry.' Frequently, this requires denying your own requirements and desires. A dysfunctional heart chakra could result in physical symptoms such as heart palpitations, chest sensations, high or low blood pressure, and poor blood circulation.

How can the heart chakra be healed and balanced?

There are numerous methods for healing the heart chakra, but an imbalance in this chakra is frequently caused by an imbalance in one of your lower chakras. Especially if your heart chakra is overactive, it could be a sign that you lack a defined life purpose or at least a sense of autonomy and freedom to make your own decisions. If you find yourself being extremely negative or cynical toward others, you can attempt to soften your heart by taking a stroll through nature or sitting in the shade of a large tree while a gentle breeze dances around you. To radiate love toward others and to open the petals of your heart chakra, you must embrace yourself and your true essence as valuable and necessary for this planet, and you must feel how interconnected we are. As a first step in this direction, you can define your needs and acknowledge that you have a right to them – that acting in accordance with your needs is neither futile nor selfish. The greatest gift you can bestow upon humanity is the genuine expression of your authentic self.

Asanas to restore the heart chakra:

Our vulnerability can result in painful experiences, but it is also the source of our greatest reserves of inner fortitude and bravery.

Camel posture. This pose is designed to expose your vulnerability and make you more receptive to receiving affection by opening your chest. Begin by kneeling on the floor with your knees approximately hip-width apart. Press the soles of your feet into the ground and allow your weight to be absorbed by the Earth. Place your hands on your bottom, inhale deeply, and draw your shoulder blades together as you move your torso forwards. Then, you can reach your fingertips to your ankles while keeping your chest open and your heart pointing to the heavens. If you experience lower back discomfort, do not overextend and only go as deeply as is comfortable. Hold this position while you take several deep breaths.

Child position. Contradict this position by adopting a child's pose. Slowly release your arms, place them over your head as you exhale, and then position them on the floor in front of you as you sit on your heels with your big toes touching the floor. Exhale as you position your abdomen below your ankles. Reach your hands forward with fingertips spread, reconnect with your breath, and hold this pose for as long as it is comfortable.

Meditation

For the heart chakra, you can attempt a guided meditation that aligns your consciousness with the heart. Start by taking a deep inhalation and bringing the thumb and index finger of each hand together to form a circle. Place the left hand on the left knee and the right hand directly above the solar plexus in the center of the thorax. Visualize your heart chakra, which is located at the base of your vertebra and at heart level. Begin by mentally honoring your heart for nourishing every part of your body as you breathe in and out. Then, visualize your heart as a person and attempt to communicate with it; ask it what its needs would be if it were an actual person and what would make it happiest. End the practice by promising to respect the desires and requirements of your heart. Additionally, you can chant the sound of the heart chakra, YAM. The more frequently you engage in this practice, you may find it simpler to identify the authentic needs of your true self and to make more effective decisions that respect those needs.

Diet & Nutrition

Green vegetables are beneficial for regulating the heart chakra. The next time you boil pasta, try adding some spinach fronds or that childhood favorite, broccoli. You can also try substituting avocado for butter or margarine as a condiment for your sandwiches. Lettuce, asparagus, and broad beans are all excellent side dishes, as are nutritious green beverages.

Chakras And Energy Channel Varieties

There have been numerous references to energy channels throughout the text, but what exactly are these channels? This will be discussed in depth in this chapter.

In a person's body, there are three categories of energy channels known as energy shafts. The spine is the origin of these fibers in humans. The central position contains an energy channel known as the Shushumna. Pingala and Ida are the names of the two other energy channels that travel parallel to the central one. Ida is on the left side of Shushumna, while Pingala is on its right. These three energy shafts travel parallel to a person's spine in the larger context. The issue now is how these shafts contribute to the formation of chakras.

The answer is straightforward. Chakras manifest where these three categories of energy channels converge and begin ascending the spinal cord.

Chakras are responsible for collecting Prana, or life force energy. Then, they transmute Prana's energy into other forms and distribute it to other parts of the body. Many of us continue to be misled regarding the significance of chakras to our mortal bodies. Generally, it is believed that chakras serve only spiritual health or the psyche. However, they are equally essential for a person's physical appearance. They contribute to the transmission of energy, as mentioned previously. Without chakras, it would be impossible to transfer energy from one point to another, and the material body of a person would not be possible. This is why the obstruction of energy channels causes ailment or disease.

Moreover, chakras are associated with specific body regions and organs. They have an effect on these organs and provide vitality to this body part. Therefore, chakras allow the human body to function adequately by assisting organs in carrying out their duties effectively. In addition, it is essential to consider that every organ is connected to the brain and that mental health is dependent on physical health. Our spiritual wellbeing is connected to our mental health. Therefore, everything is interconnected and interdependent. Each organ in the human body corresponds to a spiritual point or organ form. The condition of mortal organs affects their immortal counterparts. Chakras, or energy centers, are difficult to comprehend due to the fact that each individual has his own chakras, whose shape and performance differ from person to person. One shoe does not suit all feet. To comprehend the chakras of each individual, a minor adjustment is required. When performing certain exercises to activate the chakras, caution must be taken, and experts must be cautious. Chakras also influence a person's conduct. For instance, if a person's energy channel associated with self-confidence is blocked, that person will always feel low and terrible about his work. He will experience desolation, and his emotions will dominate his thoughts. Therefore, he will be extremely aggressive towards those who are satisfied with themselves and their task.

Chakras are known to vibrate at a frequency required by the human body. Their activity and vibration vary between individuals. Les chakras in the lower positions vibrate less than those in the upper positions. The frequency of vibration at the lower level is lower because the lower level chakras are associated with an individual's emotions. Lower level chakras have a larger density than higher level chakras. On the other hand, higher-level chakras emit a higher frequency because they are associated with the mind and intellect.

The health of a person's chakras is essential to their physical health. Chakras offer balance to our lives, and their absence results in illness, which can lead to death because it is impossible to survive without energy. It is evident that people depend on yoga for both their physical and spiritual health. The reason for this is due to the fact that yoga improves the health of our chakras. In actuality, yoga is performed to refine a person's chakras. In yoga, practitioners attempt to restore balance to their chakras and transfer the lower chakras to the higher ones. This indicates that they attempt to activate their higher chakras through yoga and meditation. This assists them in bringing spirituality and physical form into harmony. People who practice yoga are able to discover their inner peace and access their internal space. After creating internal space, a person becomes more conscientious of how he spends his energy. This realization aids in maintaining a check on one's conduct, which ultimately improves one's interactions with others in society. This enables an individual to regulate his energy on his own.

Harmonizing the upper and lower level energies is a crucial concept in this context. This can be grasped using Maslow's hierarchy of needs. Maslow presented a model illustrating a pyramid of requirements. The lowest level of the pyramid represented the need for sustenance, followed by another level, and so on until the highest level of self-actualization. According to the hypothesis he presented, once a person's basic needs are met, he or she attempts to satisfy higher-level needs. Similarly, chakras enable a person to ascend from lesser to higher energy levels. The final stage is the crown, which represents the pinnacle of spirituality.

As the energies at higher levels are less dense than those at lower levels, it is necessary to achieve a balance between the two. Every level of energy has a counterpart on every other level, which is an important point to note. For example, the seventh level corresponds to the first level, and the sixth level to the second. This aids in refining the energies to the point where a balance is achieved between them.

Third Chakra

Moving up in the body, the third chakra, also called Manipura, is represented as a triangle pointing down, circumscribed by a circle with ten petals along its exterior. The color associated with this Manipura is yellow, so anything matching the color, from food to clothes, is able to help increase energy levels or remove existing blockage.

The Manipura is located between the sternum (breastbone) and the stomach and is also referred to as the solar plexus. This position means that it is able to directly influence the digestive system, and even metabolism. The importance of this chakra is highlighted by the fact that at its level the body obtains energy from the digested food. Any disturbances are reflected in the body's poor capacity of using the external resources, thus limiting the ability to heal and replace damaged cells. Physical problems revolve around all sorts of digestive problems, among which ulcers, liver problems, constipation, parasites, colitis, food allergies, abnormal high or low sugar levels in the blood are the most frequent. As a side fact, Manipura was traced down with accuracy inside the human body and it is believed that it resides in a group of pancreatic cells called Islets of Langerhans.

Unanimously, the third chakra is regarded as the center of personal power, the location from which the ego is inflated and explosive emotions are released. Anything motivated by passion, impulse, or wrath is infused with Manipura energy. Individuals with excessive amounts of this energy who are unable to transfer it to other chakras typically experience anxiety and irritability. These states typically progress to full-scale, uncontrollable outbursts of rage, typically directed at others, leaving the body in a state of mental exhaustion. Lack of confidence, perplexity, and even depression can significantly impair a person's quality of life. Restoring equilibrium at this level restores self-respect and the desire to accept new challenges, making the individual more gregarious and extroverted.

Chakras And Glands

There appears to be no direct correlation between glands and chakras in traditional Indian chakra systems. Modern literature from both Western and Eastern cultures emphasizes the relationship between each of the primary chakras and the endocrine, nervous, and organ systems.

Two Western figures began to imply, per Patricia Mercier's "The Chakra Bible," that the position of the seven primary chakras coincides with the locations of nerve plexi, endocrine glands, and organs. Leadbeater, one of the first Westerners to cast light on the chakra system, and Alice Bailey, a theosophist and teacher of esoteric knowledge at the turn of the 20th century, both began outlining the relationships between the chakras and the human body's physiology.

How Chakras and Glands Interrelate

Disturbances in the subtle energy flowing through the chakras manifest as physical manifestations and symptoms associated with the corresponding glands and organs. Chakras are not corporeal or physiological in nature. They are considered energy centers that influence our physical and biological being on multiple levels.

When one of our energy centers is forced out of balance by a blockage, it is possible for physical ailments to occur. It is essential to remember that chakras operate according to the same principle as a pendulum. If one of them is underactive or overactive, evidence will manifest that it is "out of rhythm." Chakra balancing is necessary.

The disturbance is either sensed at the level of that particular chakra or at the level of another chakra or set of chakras that are connected to it. When the throat chakra is blocked, for instance, you may experience sore throat, neck discomfort, or laryngitis. Similarly, excessive blood pressure and heart-related issues can occur when the heart chakra is out of balance.

Pituitary Gland Meridian

Pituitary gland chakra and pineal gland chakra are two chakra organs that regulate overall glandular and biological function.

The primary function of the pituitary gland is to regulate body chemistry. This pea-sized gland located between the eyes regulates emotion and intellect and collaborates with the pineal gland to attain overall balance.

Pineal Gland Center

In essence, the pineal gland regulates and (when necessary) inhibits pituitary gland function. The balancing of these two glands contributes to the emergence of the Third Eye.

Heart Chakra and the Thymus Gland

The Heart chakra or Anahata is the chakra associated with the thymus gland. It is situated at the level of the collar bones in the middle of the thorax. It is a beneficial area to regulate in chakra healing because it influences the state of the nervous system and helps calm agitation.

A straightforward technique for interacting with the thymus gland is to lightly tap with the tips of your fingers on the center of the chest, at the level of the collar bones, or on each side of the chest, approximately 3 to 4 inches away. The first technique tends to calm the nervous system, while the second increases the level of vitality. You should investigate EFT...Emotional Freedom Technique; I'll elaborate on this later.

Chapter 9 - Sahasrara Chakra

"You are never alone. Everyone is eternally connected to you."
~ Amit Ray

Namaste, and light and love! Where are all my ultra-spiritual New Age friends? The seventh and final energy center of our voyage, the Crown or Sahasrara Chakra, is your home and comfort zone. Our very own infinite thousand-petal lotus. At the Sahasrara Chakra's infinite lotus, we progress beyond the visible color spectrum. This is the entire range of colors and energies. If you must assign it a name, call it indigo that is pure white. So much of what the Crown is about is beyond words, but I'll do my best to give you a sense of this magnificent energy through words.

Understanding is the basis of the Crown Chakra, but not just on an intellectual level. Actually, not at all on an intellectual level. And I know that some of you will struggle with this because you will want it to make intellectual logic, but it won't! In fact, the Crown is beyond description, making it difficult for me to write this chapter. When your chakras are healthy, the energy is flowing as it should, and there is a connection between the Root and Crown chakras, you begin to comprehend what I mean when I say it is beyond words. Those of you who recognize this connection will be nodding and saying "yes." Some yoga organizations refer to it as satchidananda. Buddhists may term it samadhi. Bliss. Self-realization. Heaven. Enlightenment. The Crown rests atop the Sushumna Nadi, the central energy channel I mentioned. The Ida and Pingala meet at Ajna, the location of common human consciousness. Here, we transcend!

The Crown is where we surpass the limitations of human intelligence and comprehension. When we are unbalanced at the Crown, we have difficulty trusting the large picture, and we desire to know, control, and comprehend everything. The problem arises because so much of what we wish to comprehend is beyond the comprehension of the human intellect. It cannot be explained by logic. Science has no explanation. Yet, we attempt to fit it into a tidy explanation that fits our cognitive abilities. This creates further separation! We essentially perpetuate a cycle of insanity by pursuing knowledge and control.

I speak from personal experience. I did it!

Sahasrara is our true spiritual center; it is the portal that transports us beyond human consciousness, which explains why the most spiritually advanced among us prefer to reside here. It's amazing when everything is spiritual and mystical! Trust me, I get it. It is significantly more appealing than the heavy, dense matter of the Earth domain. But residing in a Crown that is too expansive is also unhealthy. We must respect the temple bestowed to us in the form of our physical body. In the name of spirituality, dishonoring and harming one's body is not spiritual.

Sahasrara's energy assists the Ajna in pattern recognition and in comprehending and integrating all of the knowledge and wisdom we acquire along the path of life. Consequently, when there is a blockage or imbalance in this area, we struggle to make sense of a chaotic and disordered existence. This may explain why so many of us struggle to recognize and learn from our own detrimental patterns. It is essential to realize that working with the Sahasrara is nearly pointless without simultaneously developing and healing the Muladhara, as true expansion and comprehension cannot occur without the support of profound roots in the Earth.

Throughout our human existence, we struggle so intensely with attachment issues due to energetic imbalances in the Crown. We are attached to persons, places, things, events, and times. We cling because we need something to give us depth, something to occupy the void that arises when we are disconnected from the Sahasrara energy - our own divinity. As do the other diverse schools of yoga, the schools of self-realization and Kriya Yoga aim to illuminate a path to self-awareness. Authentic yoga is the voyage through the self to the self, which means we arrive at self-realization, not in the sense of the physical self, but in the sense of the higher self, or Christ Consciousness, as Yogananda termed it.

Sahasrara energy governs our fundamental Right to Know, Learn, and Understand. Do you believe that you have the access to knowledge and education? Or do you keep your head down and play the role of an obedient person who finds it more convenient to avoid paying attention or seeking knowledge? Do you believe that the world of knowledge and information belongs to those other than yourself? When education does not encourage curiosity (as so many modern systems do), the Crown's vitality can become unbalanced. Humans are inquisitive. This is how we acquire knowledge. Punishing curiosity deprives us of the right to know and learn.

The Essence

"The basic fallacy of humanity is to believe that I am here and you are there."
-Yasutani Roshi

The Crown Chakra is located in the area of the cranium known as the fontanel, which is soft until shortly after birth, when the skull plates fuse. This chakra is where the finite (mind, ego) and the infinite (soul, unadulterated essence, Divinity) meet. From this perspective, we can comprehend reality as it is, rather than through the hazy filters of our intellect, emotions, and ego. Consider that the Third Eye is where we see, and the Crown is where we comprehend what we see. When obstructed at the Crown, we cannot comprehend what we see.

Keep in mind, however, that we are discussing something that is beyond intellectual comprehension. Those who are obstructed at the Crown contend with over-intellectualization because they are attempting to force an understanding with the rational brain rather than the higher mind.

Working with the Crown Chakra may be beneficial if you frequently experience a lack of grounding and if you have lofty aspirations but are unable to manifest them. So many great ideas and inspirations originate from deep within "the mind." Call it the higher self, consciousness, or the Source if you like, but these ideas originate from somewhere. When the energy is properly flowing through the body, we are able to incorporate these inspirations into actual projects, duties, and creations. This is impossible if we only reside in "the clouds" of the highest chakras, particularly the Crown.

We have all been that person, or we know one, who floats through life 'in flow' doing whatever they (or we) feel compelled to do. Oftentimes, these people (we) have great ideas about what we can offer the world, but because of the disconnect between Root and Crown, we cannot establish a stable enough environment for these ideas to flourish.

Sahasrara is the center of illumination, interconnectedness, comprehension, and purity. Sahasrara provides us with purpose and direction in life. It is the conduit through which the Higher Self's guidance, wisdom, insight, and clarity are transmitted to the conscious mind. As you strive to open Sahasrara and get energy flowing, you may discover that your clarity, consciousness, and innate sense of well-being sharpen significantly. My favorite aspect of perceiving the world through the energy of a balanced Sahasrara Chakra is the sense of awe and amazement that even the simplest of things inspire. Have you ever been filled with awe and gratitude for the majesty of a mountain range or a sunset? Or viewed a child being a child or nature doing what nature does and been profoundly moved by the awe-inspiring nature of life and the world? That is the essence of your Crown Chakra.

Positivity of Sahasrara manifests in the capacity to experience gratitude, unity, oneness, and connection with all beings. It consists of Divine affection, harmony, and modesty. Here, we begin to understand that the concept of the self is an illusion created by the ego-mind. As we work with this energy, our need for possessions and attachments diminishes because we realize on a practical level that objects cannot purchase happiness. When we make the connection, everything falls into position, and what was once intellectual knowledge becomes genuine comprehension and wisdom.

Negative characteristics include attachment to material possessions, separation from the psyche and spiritual path, and emptiness. This typically manifests as a dearth of meaning. Apathy. Emptiness. The search for meaning in life is motivated by the desire to investigate and comprehend spiritual expansion and development. Thus, one of the worst things you can do for yourself is to settle into a comfortable position in life that never challenges you to leave your comfort zone.

Reflect on yourself:

Do you find yourself living in complete ignorance of spiritual matters?

Are you cynical and skeptical of all meaning?

Do you feel like your life lacks direction and purpose?

Do you frequently experience euphoria and joy?

As I have worked to develop my connection and the energy of the Crown, I have discovered that nothing can shake my inner conviction that everything is unfolding as it should and that I am exactly where I am intended to be, regardless of what occurs. I no longer attempt to impose my will on everything; instead, I am content to trust the process. Even when I am frustrated or irritated, I recognize that there is a larger picture at play, and I have faith in that larger picture.

I also recognize that there is a profound connection between all living things that cannot be rationally and intellectually explained. Yes! You see? I reside in a location where BOTH are viable. I can be triggered and observe myself in that space, while recognizing that the trigger is for my growth in the context of a greater whole. I may still succumb to the trigger and yell, weep, or scream because I am human and perhaps I must confront and experience that thing in order to evolve. And because I COMPREHEND, I permit it to occur.

C'mon. That is quite impressive, right? Imagine having such a high level of comprehension and awareness.

You can.

I used to be extremely rigid in my thinking and beliefs, and I was extremely critical of everyone, including myself. I spent my time and energy comparing myself to everyone, constantly oscillating between being superior to and inferior to them. I judged those who were living and succeeding in life out of bitterness, anger, and self-loathing, and I judged those who were screwing up their lives worse than I was to feed my delusion that my life wasn't that terrible! I believed it was my responsibility to act as judge, juror, and executioner for everyone I did not comprehend. Now I understand, with humility, that it is not my responsibility to comprehend the reasoning behind every action here. NOT I AM GOD!

Repeat after me!

NOT I AM GOD!

Be appreciative because they have their duties

They have their work cut out for them.

Simply be yourself and enjoy the journey.

For those of you unfamiliar with my background, I was addicted to IV cocaine and heroin, homeless, and committing offenses to support my habits. I was living on the outskirts of society, so I was in no position to judge anyone... However, if we look for individuals to judge, we will always find them. There will always be someone ahead of us and someone behind us that we can compare ourselves to at any given time. Because of this, it is crucial to have connection, comprehension, and trust in the present moment. This also gives us permission to accept that even if we cannot intellectually comprehend another person's choices, we do not need to. It is not our place to condemn, sentence, and execute others. When we attain a deeper comprehension, we do so in a manner that defies description.

The purpose of engaging with Sahasrara is to establish a genuine connection, unity, and oneness with all beings; to recognize that we are all identical. There is no distinction, and there is no separation. Duality dissipates as we work with this energy because we attain this superior comprehension. Our opinions become merely that — opinions, not our identities. We see in order to comprehend, not to condemn. We seek to love as opposed to divide. Sahasrara has a strong connection to integration and equilibrium; it is where we transform our knowledge and experiences into wisdom.

Sahasrara is the realization that while we are in our physical form, we are limited, but at the same time, we have limitless spiritual power to bring about whatever we desire in our lives. What a paradox! Sahasrara is the gateway to samadhi, the condition of enlightenment and liberation from all pain and enslavement. When energy is flowing through the Crown Chakra, we are able to free ourselves from the Crown demon, attachment, and cease causing our own suffering. We begin to embrace and tolerate impermanence.

So you can see that we've come full circle, correct? Can you see how a connection at the Crown is necessary for trust at the most fundamental level? We must be rooted and connected at the Root in order to comprehend and have faith in the larger picture that we access through higher consciousness. This explains why so many spiritual teachers have severe control issues. Or, as they acquire influence over others, their lack of trust stemming from the disconnection at the Root seeps in and drives them to greed, control, or manipulation. I have witnessed this firsthand. Those who fell prey to this type of imbalance are those who may be deficient in the Root and expansive in the Crown.

www.ingramcontent.com/pod-product-compliance
Lightning Source LLC
Chambersburg PA
CBHW050239120526
44590CB00016B/2153